A Girl Named
Helen Keller

In memory of my father,
John C. Hover,
who struggled to hear
—M.L.

To Jean Marzollo
—I.T.

Text copyright © 1995 by Margo Lundell.
Illustrations copyright © 1995 by Irene Trivas.

All rights reserved. Published by Scholastic Inc.
SCHOLASTIC, CARTWHEEL BOOKS, and associated logos
are trademarks and/or registered trademarks of Scholastic Inc.
Lexile is a registered trademark of MetaMetrics, Inc.

Library of Congress Cataloging-in-Publication Data is available.

ISBN-13: 978-0-590-47963-9
ISBN-10: 0-590-47963-6

30 29 28 27   14 15 16 17/0

Printed in the U.S.A. 40 • This edition first printing, April 2008

A Girl Named
Helen Keller

by Margot Lundell
Illustrated by Irene Trivas

Cartwheel
·B·O·O·K·S·®

SCHOLASTIC INC.
New York Toronto London Auckland Sydney
Mexico City New Delhi Hong Kong Buenos Aires

Chapter 1

The summer was hot.

The year was 1880.

Way down south

in a little town

in Alabama,

a healthy baby girl was born.

Her parents loved her dearly.

Her name was Helen Keller.

Then the baby became ill.

She was not yet two years old.

Day after day her fever was high.

The servants tried to help.

Her parents tried to help.

The doctor shook his head.

"There is nothing more we can do,"
he said.

"The baby may not live."

Helen lived.
But she was not the same
after her illness.
"Something is very wrong,"
her mother said.
At last they found out the truth.
The child was deaf and blind.

The baby grew into a little girl.

Her parents felt sorry for her.

Helen often cried

and held on to her mother.

"Give the poor child what she wants,"

her father would say.

Helen was deaf and blind,
but she was bright, too.
She copied everyone.
Sometimes she made herself
look like her father.
She put on his glasses
and held up his newspaper.

Some people did not think
Helen could learn anything.
Her mother did not agree.
"Helen is very smart," she said.
"But how can we reach her?
She is locked up inside of herself."

Chapter 2

Helen began to grow wild.
She would not let anyone
comb her hair.
Her clothes were always dirty.

Helen often became angry.
Sometimes she lay on the floor
and kicked her feet.

Then a baby sister was born.

Helen was not happy.

"My poor Helen," said her mother.

"Now there is always a baby in my lap."

One day Helen pushed the baby
out of its cradle onto the floor.
"No, Helen!" her mother cried.
"What will we do?
We must find help."

The Kellers went to Washington, D.C., to
visit the famous Alexander Graham Bell.
Maybe he could help Helen.
Dr. Bell had invented the telephone.
He was also a teacher of the deaf.
"Helen can learn," said Dr. Bell.
"But she will need a special teacher.
Write to the Perkins School
for the Blind in Boston,
Massachusetts.
Ask them to send a teacher."

Helen's father wrote to the school.

Soon he had an answer.

"Thank goodness!" he said.

"The Perkins School will send a teacher."

Chapter 3

On the afternoon of March 3, 1887,
the teacher arrived.
Helen was standing near the
front door of the house.
Suddenly she felt footsteps
on the stairs.
She thought it was her mother
and reached out.

Someone took Helen's hand
and pulled her close.
It was not Helen's mother,
so the girl pulled away.
It was Anne Sullivan, her teacher.
She was the young woman from Boston
who had come to show Helen the world.
And she was the woman who had come
to love her.
Later in her life, Helen would call this
day the birthday of her soul.

On the day she arrived,
Miss Sullivan gave Helen a doll.
"D-o-l-l spells doll,"
said Miss Sullivan.
She spelled the word with her fingers
into Helen's hand.
She made the letters
with a special alphabet.
It was an alphabet of
hand signs.

Helen copied her teacher.
She spelled d-o-l-l.
But she did not understand
what she was doing.

Soon Miss Sullivan found out
that Helen did just what she wanted.
At dinner Helen would not sit
in a chair.
She walked around the table.
She ate from everyone's plate.
And she ate with her fingers.
"You are not being kind to Helen,"
Miss Sullivan told the family.
"She must be taught how to behave."

There were terrible fights.

"Helen, you will do it *my* way!"

Miss Sullivan shouted,

even though Helen couldn't hear her.

She made Helen sit in a chair.

Helen stood up again.

She made Helen hold a spoon.

Helen threw the spoon away.

She made Helen eat

from her own plate.

Helen threw the plate

across the room.

Every meal was a fight.
But Miss Sullivan began to win.
Helen sat in a chair at last.

Helen's mother worried about Helen.
"Miss Annie, you are too hard
on her," Mrs. Keller said.
Miss Sullivan was firm.
"I cannot teach Helen
unless I can control her."

Miss Sullivan spoke to Mr. Keller.
"I must be alone with Helen
for a while," she said.
"May we move into the little house
in the garden?"
"For two weeks," said Mr. Keller.
"No more."

The Kellers took Helen
for a long ride.
Then they took her to the little
house in the garden.
That way Helen did not know
she was close to home.

Chapter 4

Miss Sullivan was strict but kind.

Helen began to like her.

In the little house Miss Sullivan

spelled words for Helen day and night.

b-e-a-d-s — beads

d-o-g — dog

f-u-r — fur

Helen spelled the words

back to her teacher.

But she still did not understand

what she was doing.

"Helen, the words mean something!"

said Miss Sullivan.

She was begging Helen to understand.

The two weeks were up.
Helen and Miss Sullivan moved back
into the big house.
Helen still did not understand
the hand signs.
But her teacher did not give up.
One day she was teaching the words
w-a-t-e-r and m-u-g.
Helen mixed up the words
again and again.
"We need a rest," said Miss Sullivan.
"We will take a walk outside."

The day was warm and sunny.

Helen and her teacher

walked in the garden.

They came to the water pump.

Miss Sullivan had an idea.

The teacher began pumping.

Water poured out.

Miss Sullivan put Helen's hand

in the water.

Then she spelled w-a-t-e-r.

"Water, Helen! W-a-t-e-r!"

Suddenly Helen understood.

She understood that w-a-t-e-r meant
the wet something running over her hand.

She understood that "water" was a word.

She understood that words were
the most important thing in the world.

Words would tell her everything
she wanted to know.

"My heart began to sing,"
she later wrote.

"It was as if I had come back to life
after being dead."

Suddenly Helen wanted to know
the name of everything.
g-r-o-u-n-d — ground
f-l-o-w-e-r — flower
Then she pointed to Miss Sullivan.
Miss Sullivan spelled out...
t-e-a-c-h-e-r — teacher.

Miss Sullivan knew now
that Helen understood.
She was filled with joy.
"I thought my heart would burst,"
she wrote.

Miss Sullivan ran to the house with Helen.
She told everyone what had happened.
Helen's mother wept with joy.
"My darling child," she cried.
Then Mrs. Keller turned to Helen's teacher.
"Miss Annie, what you have done
is a miracle!"

It was true.

A miracle *did* happen that day.

But it was not the last one.

The life of Helen Keller was filled

with miracles for years to come.

Helen Keller 1880–1968

In the years that followed,
Helen learned to read and write.
She even learned to speak.
She went to school.
She graduated from Radcliffe College
with honors.
Anne Sullivan helped Helen
all through school.
They stayed together
almost fifty years.
They stayed together
until Teacher died.

In her life Helen wrote five books.

She traveled many places.

She met kings and presidents.

She spoke to groups of people around the world.

Most of the work she did was

to help people who were blind or deaf.

She was a warm, caring person.

People loved her in return.

The life of Helen Keller brought hope to many.

The One-Hand Manual Alphabet

T H E   E N D